United States Presidents
And Great Americans

Illustrations By
Mark Nelson

Story By
Glen Ritter

Printed in the United States. All rights reserved.
Copyright 1994

Published by
Pyramid Publishing
P.O. Box 129
Zenda, Wisconsin
53195

First President of the United States

George Washington, 1789–1797

Revolutionary War leader and hero. The father of our country.

Second President of the United States
John Adams, 1797–1801
First president to live in the White House. A renowned diplomat.

Third President of the United States
Thomas Jefferson, 1801–1809
Author of The Declaration of Independence, and responsible
for obtaining the treaty for the purchase of Louisiana.

Fourth President of the United States
James Madison, 1809–1817
Star-Spangled Banner written and White House burned by the British during his term. Dolley Madison was a renowned White House hostess.

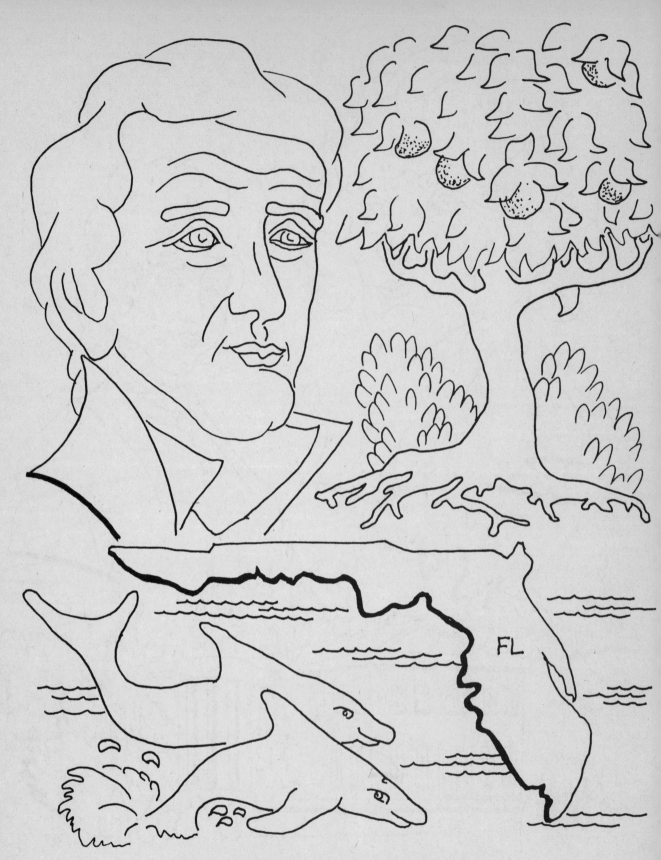

Fifth President of the United States
James Monroe, 1817–1825
Florida was purchased from Spain. Pronouncement of the independence
of the Western Hemisphere (the Monroe Doctrine).

Sixth President of the United States
John Quincy Adams, 1825–1829
Only son of a president to become president. The Erie Canal was opened.

Seventh President of the United States
Andrew Jackson, 1829–1837
American frontiersman nicknamed "Old Hickory." While president
he strengthened the federal government over the states.

Eighth President of the United States
Martin Van Buren, 1837–1841
Served as a U.S. senator and vice president before being elected.
The first great depression took place during his term of office.

Ninth President of the United States
William Henry Harrison, 1841
Served in both houses of Congress prior to his election.
He died of pneumonia one month after his inauguration.

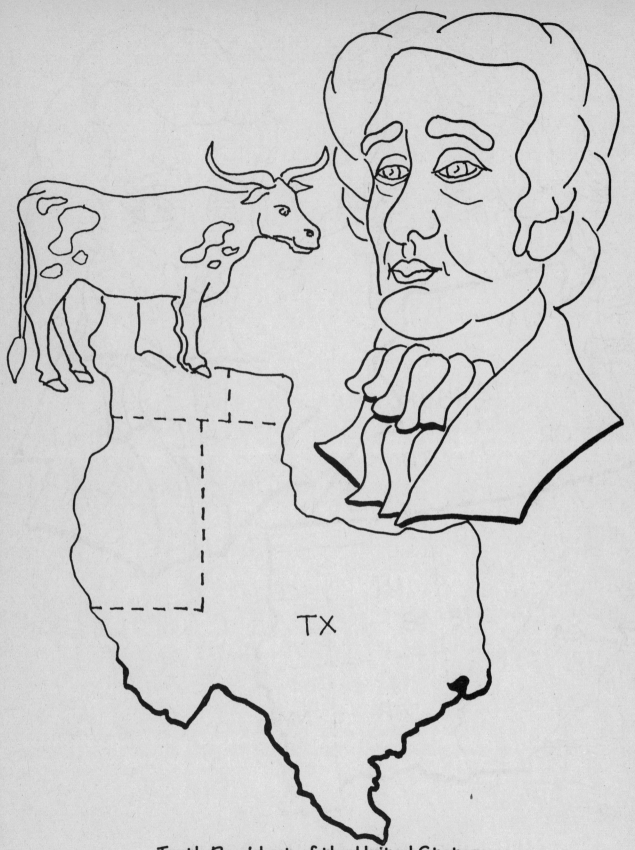

TX

Tenth President of the United States
John Tyler, 1841–1845
Served in both houses of Congress prior to his election. He believed
in territorial expansion, and Texas was annexed during his term.

Eleventh President of the United States

James Polk, 1845–1849

A westward expansionist. The land forming nine of our West and
Northwest states was added to the United States.

Twelfth President of the United States
Zachary Taylor, 1849–1850
Well-known military man nicknamed "Old Rough and Ready."
Western gold rush during his term. Died after one year in office.

Thirteenth President of the United States
Millard Fillmore, 1850–1853
Became president after the death of Zachary Taylor.
He opened up trade with Japan.

Fourteenth President of the United States
Franklin Pierce, 1853–1857
Responsible for the Gladstone Purchase, and advanced
Atlantic crossings by ship and construction of the continental railroad.

Fifteenth President of the United States
James Buchanan, 1857–1861
North and South started to divide over slavery and states' rights.
He believed government should not interfere with secession.

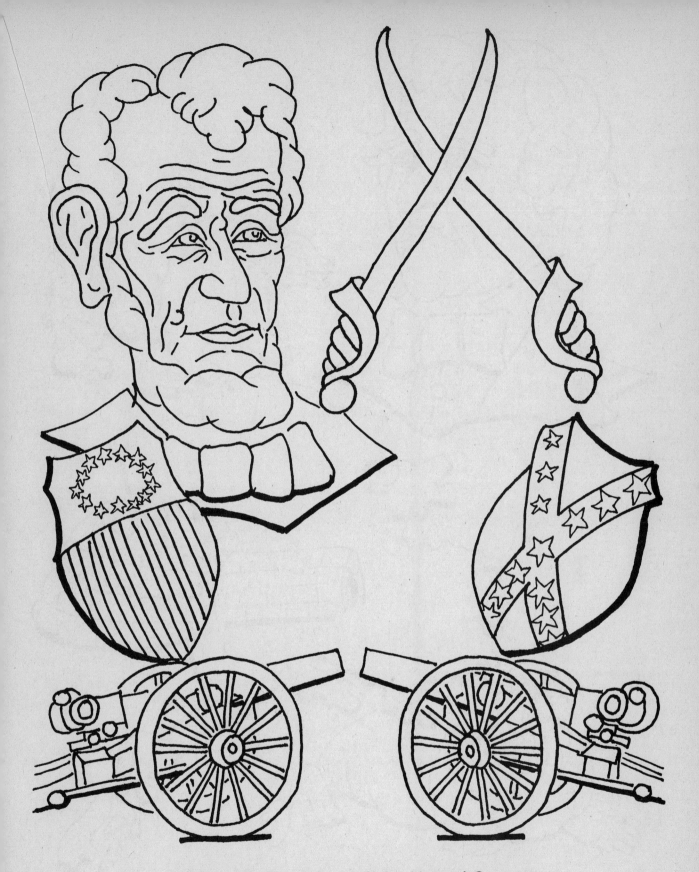

Sixteenth President of the United States
Abraham Lincoln, 1861–1865
Civil War began. He believed the nation could not endure half slave and half free. "With malice toward none, with charity for all."

Seventeenth President of the United States
Andrew Johnson, 1865–1869
Carried out Lincoln's reconstruction plan for the South.
He negotiated the purchase of Alaska from Russia.

Eighteenth President of the United States
Ulysses S. Grant, 1869–1877
Famous Civil War general who accepted the surrender of the South
by General Lee. The "Golden Spike" joined the continental railroads.

Nineteenth President of the United States
Rutherford B. Hayes, 1877–1881
Believed in civil reform of government. He ended the government's occupation of the Southern states. Reconstruction of the South.

Twentieth President of the United States

James A. Garfield, 1881

A general in the Civil War. He restored power and dignity
to the White House. Assassinated his first year in office.

Twenty-First President of the United States
Chester Arthur, 1881–1885
Known for his honesty and efficiency. The Brooklyn Bridge and
first steel skyscraper were built during his term.

Twenty-Second and Twenty-Fourth President of the United States

Grover Cleveland, 1885–1889, 1893–1897

Served two non-consecutive terms of office. The Statue of Liberty was given to America by France. Use of cameras became widespread.

Twenty-Third President of the United States
Benjamin Harrison, 1889–1893
Civil War general. Homesteaders stormed west for the Oklahoma land rush.
Sherman Anti-Trust Act continued governmental social control.

Twenty-Fifth President of the United States
William McKinley, 1897–1901
Sinking of the battleship Maine started the Spanish-American War.
McKinley assassinated shortly after being elected to a second term.

Twenty-Sixth President of the United States
Theodore Roosevelt, 1901–1909
Led the Rough Riders during Spanish American War.
Advocated greater governmental controls. Awarded the Nobel Peace Prize.

Twenty-Seventh President of the United States
William Taft, 1909–1913
Exploration of the North Pole was furthered. Served as Chief Justice
of the Supreme Court after leaving office.

Twenty-Eighth President of the United States
Woodrow Wilson, 1913–1921
The Lusitania was sunk by a German submarine. America entered
World War I in 1917. The League of Nations was formed.

Twenty-Ninth President of the United States
Warren Harding, 1921–1923
The "Roaring Twenties" era began. The Eighteenth Amendment (Prohibition) was adopted. The Teapot Dome scandal was disclosed.

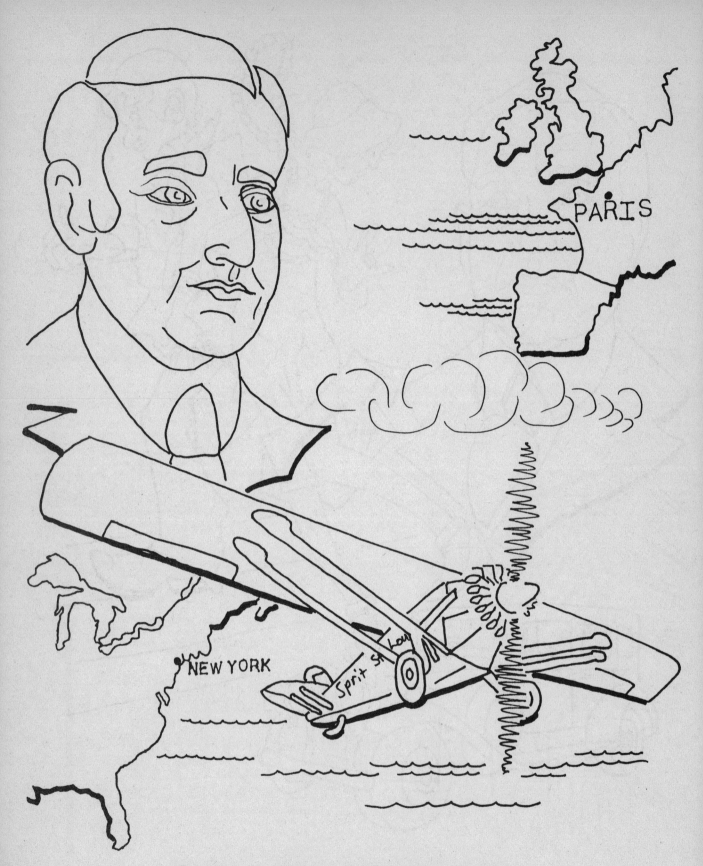

Thirtieth President of the United States
Calvin Coolidge, 1923–1929
Lindbergh flew solo across the Atlantic. Great prosperity during his term
of office. Restored faith in the office of the presidency.

Thirty-First President of the United States
Herbert Hoover, 1929–1933
The stock market crashed. The Great Depression of 1929 followed
the prosperity of the '20s. Many businesses closed.

Thirty-Second President of the United States
Franklin D. Roosevelt, 1933–1945
New Deal Legislation put into effect. America entered World War II in 1941 after the bombing of Pearl Harbor. Roosevelt died in office.

Thirty-Third President of the United States
Harry S. Truman, 1945–1953
Dropped atomic bomb, ending World War II. Helped to rebuild Europe
with the Marshall Plan. Expanded Social Security programs.

Thirty-Fourth President of the United States

Dwight D. Eisenhower, 1953–1961

While in office Interstate Highway system started and jet propulsion advanced. Strengthened the free world against Communism.

Thirty-Fifth President of the United States
John F. Kennedy, 1961–1963
Air travel became common, rocket programs advanced, and America
made plans to send a man to the moon. Assassinated while in office.

Thirty-Sixth President of the United States
Lyndon B. Johnson, 1963–1969
America became entrenched in the Vietnam War. First American walked
in space. Civil rights legislation was advanced.

Thirty-Seventh President of the United States
Richard M. Nixon, 1969–1974
The Vietnam War ended. The first man walked on the moon. Trade opened
with China. The first president to resign from office.

Thirty-Eighth President of the United States
Gerald Ford, 1974–1977
Known for his honesty and integrity. American and Russian spacecrafts
linked together in space. Viking 1 landed on Mars.

Thirty-Ninth President of the United States
James Carter, 1977–1981
Peace promoted in the Middle East by bringing the leaders of Egypt
and Israel together. His administration hurt by failing economy.

Fortieth President of the United States

Ronald Reagan, 1981–1989

National economy expanded. First woman appointed
to the U.S. Supreme Court. The space shuttle began to fly.

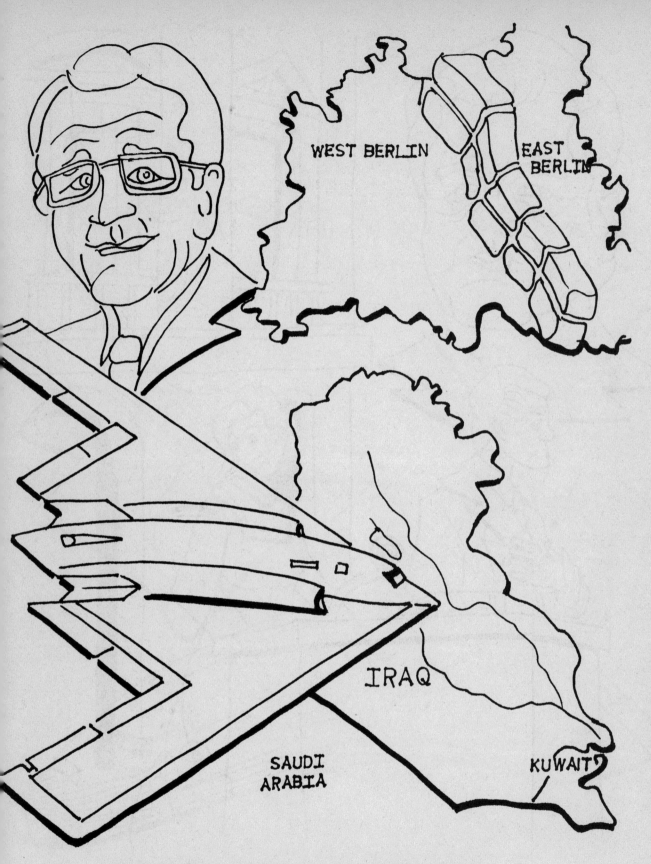

WEST BERLIN

EAST BERLIN

IRAQ

SAUDI ARABIA

KUWAIT

Forty-First President of the United States

George Bush, 1989–1993

The Berlin Wall came down. Break up of the Soviet Union. Troops sent to Kuwait to halt the Iraqi invasion (Desert Storm).

Forty-Second President of the United States
William Clinton, 1993–
Sworn into office with policy of being a New Democrat.

Benjamin Franklin, 1706–1790
Diplomat, inventor and publisher. Helped to form
the government of the United States.

Daniel Boone, 1734–1820
Famous pioneer of colonial times. He blazed the wilderness trail
through the Appalachian mountains of Kentucky.

Paul Revere, 1735–1818
Silversmith and famous American patriot. His midnight ride warned
the Continental Army at Lexington that "The British are coming."

Jean Baptiste DuSable, 1745–1818
African-American pioneer who founded the city of Chicago.
He became wealthy by trading with the Native Americans.

John Paul Jones, 1747–1792

The "Father of the American Navy." As captain of the Bonhomme Richard,
he told a British warship, "I have not yet begun to fight."

Betsy Ross, 1752–1836
Philadelphia seamstress who George Washington asked
to make the flag for the Continental Army.

Molly Pitcher, 1754–1832
Heroine of Revolutionary War. At the Battle of Monmouth she carried water for the soldiers, but soon was in position firing a cannon.

John J. Audubon, 1785–1851
One of America's greatest naturalists, best known
for his realistic paintings of birds.

Francis Scott Key, 1779–1843
Wrote the Star-Spangled Banner while being held captive during the War of 1812. The song became our national anthem in 1831.

Clara Barton, 1821–1912
A nurse during the Civil War, Barton was called the "Angel of the Battlefield."
She founded The American Red Cross.

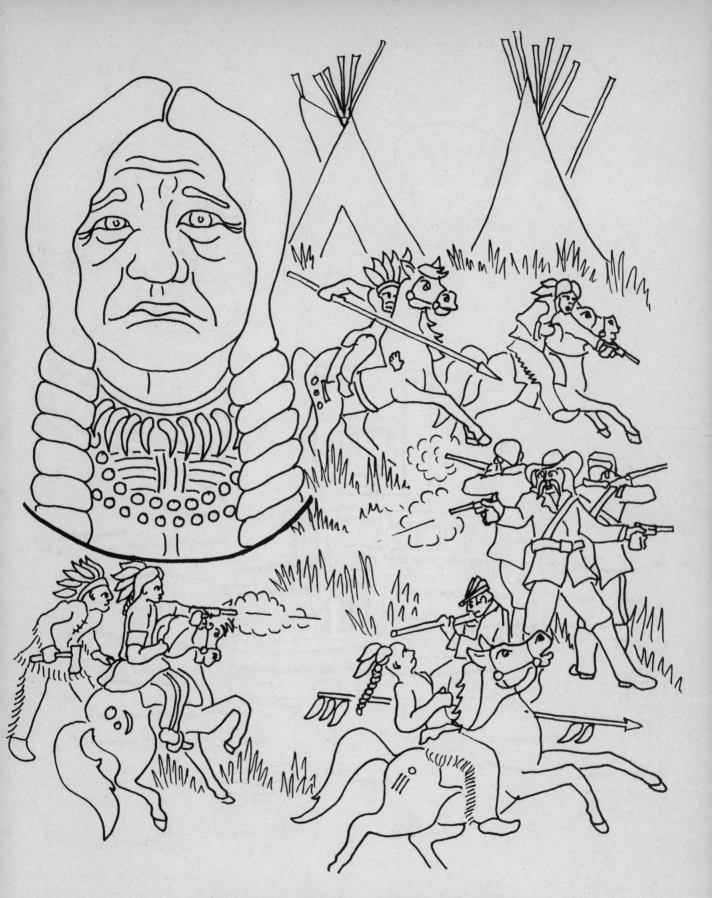

Sitting Bull, 1831–1890
Hunkpapa Sioux war chief best known for his defeat of General Custer
at the Battle of the Little Big Horn, June 1876.

Mark Twain, 1835–1910

Author of "The Adventures of Tom Sawyer" and "The Adventures of Huckleberry Finn." Considered America's best known humorist.

Alexander Graham Bell, 1847–1922
Inventor best known for the telephone. He founded and financed
an organization to help the deaf.

Thomas A. Edison, 1847–1931
America's greatest inventor. Among his many inventions were
the electric light bulb and the phonograph. He had 1,093 patents.

Henry Ford, 1863–1947

Best known for his use of the assembly line to economically produce
his Model T automobile. Several million were produced.

Wilbur Wright, 1867–1912,
and Orville Wright, 1871–1948
Inventors who designed, built and flew the first successful airplane.
It flew at Kitty Hawk, North Carolina, December 1903.

Albert Einstein, 1879–1955

One of the great scientists of all time. He was a pioneer in atomic research and discovered the Theory of Relativity.

Amelia Earhart, 1897–1937
First woman to fly solo across the Atlantic Ocean. She disappeared
while attempting to fly solo around the world.

Charles Lindbergh, 1902–1974
The first to fly solo across the Atlantic Ocean (1927), in a plane named The Spirit of St. Louis.

Martin Luther King, 1929–1968
The civil rights leader won the Nobel Peace Prize in 1964. He was assassinated before his dream for equality came true.

Neil Armstrong, 1930–
American astronaut who became the first person
to walk on the moon, July 20, 1969.

Sally Ride, 1951–
The first American woman to travel in space.